RAND NATIONAL DEFENSE RESEARCH INSTITUTE

THE RELATIONSHIP BETWEEN SEXUAL ASSAULT AND SEXUAL HARASSMENT IN THE U.S. MILITARY

Findings from the RAND Military Workplace Study

Terry L. Schell, Matthew Cefalu, Coreen Farris, Andrew R. Morral

Prepared for the DoD Sexual Assault Prevention and Response Office

For more information on this publication, visit www.rand.org/t/RR3162

Library of Congress Cataloging-in-Publication Data is available for this publication.
ISBN: 978-1-9774-0667-5

Published by the RAND Corporation, Santa Monica, Calif.
© Copyright 2021 RAND Corporation
RAND® is a registered trademark.

Support RAND
Make a tax-deductible charitable contribution at
www.rand.org/giving/contribute

www.rand.org

Preface

The Sexual Assault Prevention and Response Office within the Office of the Secretary of Defense selected the RAND Corporation to provide a new and independent evaluation of sexual assault, sexual harassment, and gender discrimination across the U.S. military. The U.S. Department of Defense (DoD) asked the RAND research team to redesign the approach used in previous DoD surveys, if changes would improve the accuracy and validity of the survey results for estimating the prevalence of sexual crimes and violations. In the summer of 2014, RAND fielded a new survey as part of the RAND Military Workplace Study.

This report describes new survey data analyses designed to identify how the sexual harassment of others in a service member's work environment affects his or her own risk of being sexually assaulted. The series that collectively describes the study methodology and its findings, to date, includes the following reports:

- *Sexual Assault and Sexual Harassment in the U.S. Military: Top-Line Estimates for Active-Duty Service Members from the 2014 RAND Military Workplace Study*
- *Sexual Assault and Sexual Harassment in the U.S. Military: Top-Line Estimates for Active-Duty Coast Guard Members from the 2014 RAND Military Workplace Study*
- *Sexual Assault and Sexual Harassment in the U.S. Military: Volume 1. Design of the 2014 RAND Military Workplace Study*
- *Sexual Assault and Sexual Harassment in the U.S. Military: Volume 2. Estimates for Department of Defense Service Members from the 2014 RAND Military Workplace Study*
- *Sexual Assault and Sexual Harassment in the U.S. Military: Annex to Volume 2. Tabular Results from the 2014 RAND Military Workplace Study for Department of Defense Service Members*
- *Sexual Assault and Sexual Harassment in the U.S. Military: Volume 3. Estimates for Coast Guard Service Members from the 2014 RAND Military Workplace Study*
- *Sexual Assault and Sexual Harassment in the U.S. Military: Annex to Volume 3. Tabular Results from the 2014 RAND Military Workplace Study for Coast Guard Service Members*
- *Sexual Assault and Sexual Harassment in the U.S. Military: Volume 4. Investigations of Potential Bias in Estimates from the 2014 RAND Military Workplace Study*

- *Sexual Assault and Sexual Harassment in the U.S. Military: Volume 5. Estimates for Installation- and Command-Level Risk of Sexual Assault and Sexual Harassment from the 2014 RAND Military Workplace Study*
- *Risk Factors for Sexual Assault and Sexual Harassment in the U.S. Military: Findings from the 2014 RAND Military Workplace Study*
- *Effects of Sexual Assault and Sexual Harassment on Separation from the U.S. Military: Findings from the 2014 RAND Military Workplace Study.*

These reports are available online at www.rand.org/surveys/rmws.

The research reported here was completed in June 2019 and underwent security review with the sponsor and the Defense Office of Prepublication and Security Review before public release.

This research was sponsored by the U.S. Department of Defense and conducted within the Forces and Resources Policy Center of the RAND National Security Research Division (NSRD), which operates the National Defense Research Institute (NDRI), a federally funded research and development center sponsored by the Office of the Secretary of Defense, the Joint Staff, the Unified Combatant Commands, the Navy, the Marine Corps, the defense agencies, and the defense intelligence enterprise.

For more information on the RAND Forces and Resources Policy Center, see www.rand.org/nsrd/frp or contact the director (contact information is provided on the webpage).

Contents

Figures and Tables

Summary

Sexual harassment and sexual assault in the military are strongly linked (Harned et al., 2002; Sadler et al., 2003). Compared with service women who did not experience sexual harassment in the past year, service women who did were 14 times more likely to indicate that they were also sexually assaulted in the past year, based on data from the 2014 RAND Military Workplace Study (RMWS) (Morral, Schell, and Gore, 2015). According to that same study, service men who were sexually harassed in the past year were almost 50 times more likely to have been sexually assaulted in the past year than were service men who had not recently experienced sexual harassment.

The observed relationship between sexual harassment and sexual assault in the military has a few plausible explanations. First, it may be an artifact of definitional overlap; that is, some sexual harassment incidents are so severe that they are also sexual assaults, and most sexual assaults in the military are by coworkers, so they would count as sexual harassment also. Second, victims of sexual harassment and sexual assault share many individual risk factors (e.g., younger age, lower pay grade, being unmarried); these common risk factors may explain the observed correlation between sexual harassment and sexual assault. Third, it could be that sexual harassment and sexual assault are manifestations of an environmental risk factor shared by coworkers, such as command climate, unit group dynamics, or local cultural norms.

In this report, we evaluate evidence of the role of environmental risk factors, using an analytic strategy that ruled out definitional overlap as an explanation for the high correlation between sexual assault and sexual harassment and that accounted for a large number of known shared individual risk factors. Nevertheless, strong associations remained between sexual assault and sexual harassment, providing some supportive evidence that environmental risk factors that are shared by coworkers contribute to both sexual harassment and sexual assault risk. Although it provides support for this hypothesis, our study was not able to identify which environmental risk factors cause the association. The deciding factor could be, for instance, a service member's command climate, the chance accumulation of perpetrators of sexual assault and sexual harassment in an environment, or cultural norms that communicate to service members that abusing others is accepted and that create graduated opportunities for offenders to learn that their behavior is unlikely to be punished. Over time, this may increase the risk that offenders' behavior will escalate from inappropriate workplace behaviors to sexual harassment and then to sexual assault.

To rule out definitional overlap and the contribution of shared risk factors in the relationship between sexual harassment and sexual assault, we first derived ambient sexual harassment rates for each service member. *Ambient* sexual harassment refers to the percentage of colleagues in their workplace who are sexually harassed; the percentage does not include any sexual harassment that the individual experiences (Glomb et al., 1997). More specifically, in our study, these rates summarize the percentage of colleagues at the unit, installation, and major command levels who were sexually harassed during the past year. By exploring the link between ambient sexual harassment—instead of personal sexual harassment—and sexual assault risk, we can be more certain that (1) an incident that was both sexual harassment and sexual assault contributes to the sexual assault rate only and is eliminated from each individual's ambient sexual harassment estimate, and (2) each service member's risk factors contribute only to his or her sexual assault risk and are largely eliminated from the ambient sexual harassment estimate. We measured ambient sexual harassment against male and female coworkers separately to allow for the possibility that harassment of men and harassment of women have differing effects on service members' sexual assault risk.

Alternatively, there could be characteristics of the workplace that increase risk of both sexual harassment and sexual assault (the third possible explanation). Candidate workplace risk factors might include weak oversight or leadership, breakdowns in good order and discipline, and a permissive attitude toward demeaning or abusive behavior. In such environments, employees may come to a shared expectation that sexual harassment is tolerated. It may be that, as workers listen to sexual joking, watch as coworkers romantically or sexually proposition others in the workplace, or hear rumors of inappropriate touching, they learn with each instance whether these behaviors are likely to be socially or professionally penalized. For those with a propensity to engage in sexual harassment, these learning opportunities provide insight into the likelihood that they too would escape social and professional sanctions. In turn, as workers learn that their harassing behaviors are accepted by those in their professional environment, there is less reason to inhibit decisions to engage in more-extreme behaviors that eventually pass the threshold to sexual assault. Consistent with this hypothesis, the U.S. Department of Defense (DoD) *2014–2016 Sexual Assault Prevention Strategy* suggests that a "unit or command where women are objectified or demeaned or inappropriate comments about race or sexual orientation go uncorrected" may create the impression that service members "may get away with other acts against women or men, including sexual assault" (DoD, 2014, p. 6). Sadler et al., 2003, reports that women who had observed their ranking officer allowing others in the unit to make sexually demeaning comments were more likely to have been sexually assaulted during their military service.

To explore whether there is other supportive evidence for this third (environmental) explanation of the relationship between sexual harassment and sexual assault risk, we pursued an analytic strategy that was designed to control for the possible effects of the first and second explanations. This allowed us to determine whether, and to what degree, the relationship between sexual harassment and sexual assault persists after accounting for definitional overlap and shared risk factors for the two events. To do so, we assessed the relationship between ambient sexual harassment and sexual assault. This approach eliminates inflation of the relationship that occurs when a single workplace event is counted as both sexual harassment and sexual assault. It also ensures that the individual's risk factors contribute to only one estimate (sexual assault) but not the other (ambient sexual harassment), which, in turn, eliminates the correlation caused by most shared individual risk factors.

We developed measures of ambient sexual harassment of service women and men using survey data on unwanted workplace experiences collected through the 2014 RMWS. The ambient sexual harassment of approximately 115,000 service members was based only on the experiences of the people they worked with (in the same unit, installation, or major command), not on their own experiences. We then used regression models to examine how ambient sexual harassment predicts each individual's sexual assault risk, over and above other known risk factors for sexual assault.

The amount of ambient sexual harassment to which members were exposed varied substantially across the units, installations, and major commands in which members of the military serve. In some such environments, only 7 percent of service women were sexually harassed in the past year; in other environments, the rate was six times higher. Ambient sexual harassment of men spanned a range from 2 percent to 17 percent across environments—an eightfold difference in risk.

Study Findings

Results of these analyses demonstrate that ambient sexual harassment against service women and men is strongly associated with risk of sexual assault, even after controlling for many other sexual assault risk factors (such as age, rank, occupation, marital status, and education level). Indeed, on average, service women's sexual assault risk increased by more than a factor of 1.5 when they worked in environments where the rates of ambient sexual harassment against women and men were above the DoD average, compared with the sexual assault risk for women working where the rates were below the DoD average. And service men's sexual assault risk increased by a factor of 1.8 when working in such environments. Both men's and women's risk of sexual assault appears to be more sensitive to the ambient sexual harassment of men than that of women, although we demonstrate that ambient sexual harassment against each gender makes independent contributions to service members' sexual assault risk.

The association between ambient sexual harassment and sexual assault risk was similar for women in each branch of service. For men, however, the association was found only in the Navy, where it was quite strong: Navy men serving in environments where the rate of ambient sexual harassment was above the DoD average had 2.0 times the risk of being sexually assaulted as Navy men serving where the rate was below the DoD average.

The association between ambient sexual harassment and sexual assault risk is not explained by other known risk factors for sexual assault that we or others have examined. In addition, it makes a unique contribution to explaining sexual assault risk over and above the most-powerful models of sexual assault risk that we previously developed (see Schell et al., forthcoming). It makes a small improvement in models of women's sexual assault risk and quite substantial improvements in models of men's sexual assault risk.

Discussion and Recommendations

We found that ambient sexual harassment is a strong predictor of sexual assault risk, over and above many other known risk factors for sexual assault. Our study ruled out the possibility that this association is due to sexual assaults also being counted as sexual harassment, and we have largely excluded the possibility that sexual assault victims have some unobserved risk factors for sexual assault that also elevate their risk of sexual harassment. Instead, it seems likely that there is a root cause of both sexual assault and sexual harassment that is found in the individual's environment, not in his or her personal or individual characteristics.

One hypothesis is that both sexual harassment and sexual assault are manifestations of the same underlying workplace disorder. When potential offenders work in environments where they observe or hear about sexual harassment occurring, see sexual harassment go unpunished, and have personal learning experiences where they participate in sexual harassment that is unpunished, they learn that mistreating colleagues is permissible in their work environment. For some, their behaviors may escalate from mistreatment that is classified as sexual harassment (e.g., repeated, upsetting sexual jokes) to abuse that is classified as sexual assault (e.g., unwanted sexual touching). As these learned expectations become shared across the workplace, a disordered workplace culture may emerge in which abuse of colleagues becomes expected as a natural or permitted occurrence.

There is reason to believe that sexual harassment and sexual assault are not the only abusive workplace behaviors that share underlying root causes (U.S. Government Accountability Office, 2017; Marquis et al., 2017). Military sexual assaults against men are often hazing-related (Jaycox et al., 2015). Similarly, the fact that service members who are sexual minorities are at substantially increased risk of sexual assault (Davis,

Vega, and McLeod, 2017) suggests that sexual assault is tied to sexual orientation discrimination. As described in an earlier report using the 2014 RMWS survey results, one-third of service members who were sexually assaulted indicated that that their perpetrator(s) sexually harassed them before the assault, and 9 percent indicated that the perpetrator(s) stalked them before the assault (Jaycox et al., 2015). Finally, in locations where sexual harassment and sexual assault of women are more common, men also face elevated risk of both. Although it is possible that workplace discrimination, harassment, hazing, assault, and stalking are related via independent causal mechanisms, it also seems plausible that they are all, at least partially, manifestations of a similar underlying cultural or workplace disorder.

In the civilian sector, sexual assault prevention programs have had disappointingly small effects on the number of sexual assaults among college students (Anderson and Whiston, 2005). It could be time to consider innovative, novel approaches to sexual assault prevention. The data presented in this report suggest that work environments in which rates of sexual harassment are high contribute to service members' risk of sexual assault. Thus, policy changes or educational efforts to reduce sexual harassment might not only limit this damaging workplace behavior but also have downstream effects on sexual assault prevalence.

Targeting inappropriate workplace behaviors as part of a strategy to prevent sexual assaults would allow DoD to focus on behaviors that are more visible and, therefore, more easily sanctioned. Inappropriate workplace behaviors and sexual harassment are more likely to occur in shared environments with witnesses or bystanders present. In contrast, sexual assaults almost all occur in private with only the victim and perpetrator present. There are many more opportunities for colleagues to deliver social sanctions that communicate the unacceptability of the sexual harassment and for supervisors and commanders to deliver professional sanctions. Because sexual harassment can span from minor, inappropriate behavior to repeated, severe sexual harassment, there are also opportunities to sanction sexual harassment while the consequences are still relatively mild and more easily delivered. That is, when a supervisor wishes to deliver a stern warning to a service member to discontinue the behavior immediately, the burden of proof is clearly lower than when the appropriate sanction would be dishonorable discharge. In addition, because sexual harassment solutions could be limited to peer-delivered social sanctions or supervisor-controlled professional sanctions, the timeline for delivery can be quite fast compared with the sanctions for sexual assault delivered by the military justice system. The likelihood that a person will learn from an event and modify his or her behavior in response to a sanction increases when the punishment occurs quickly (Schwartz, Wasserman, and Robbins, 2001), which is often more feasible in response to sexual harassment than sexual assault.

We believe that our analyses point to the promise of reducing or eliminating workplace sexual harassment as a strategy to also prevent sexual assault. This study also provides supportive evidence for DoD's policy focus on the continuum of harm in sexual assault prevention planning. The true test will come after high-quality programs or policies to improve workplace culture are delivered to a large segment of the military population; once those are in place, researchers can conduct a real-world test of the programs' and policies' influence on sexual harassment in the work environment and, finally, on sexual assault risk.

Acknowledgments

The authors wish to thank Richard Harris of the University of Texas, San Antonio, and Maria DeYoreo of the RAND Corporation for providing helpful comments and criticisms of a draft version of this report as part of RAND's quality assurance review process.

CHAPTER ONE

Introduction

Sexual harassment and sexual assault in the military are strongly linked (Harned et al., 2002; Sadler et al., 2003). Compared with service women who did not experience sexual harassment in the past year, service women who did were 14 times more likely to indicate that they were also sexually assaulted in the past year, based on data from the 2014 RAND Military Workplace Study (RMWS) (Morral, Schell, and Gore, 2015). According to that same study, service men who were sexually harassed in the past year were almost 50 times more likely to be sexually assaulted in the past year than were service men who had not recently experienced sexual harassment.

The observed relationship between sexual harassment and sexual assault in the military has a few plausible explanations. First, it could be entirely an artifact of definitional overlap. According to U.S. Department of Defense (DoD) Directive 1350.2, sexual harassment includes "physical conduct of a sexual nature" that is so severe or pervasive that "a reasonable person would perceive, and the victim does perceive, the work environment as hostile or offensive" (DoD, 2015, p. 18). DoD Directive 6495.01 summarizes the Uniform Code of Military Justice definition of sexual assault as "intentional sexual contact characterized by use of force, threats, intimidation, or abuse of authority or when the victim does not or cannot consent" (DoD, 2013, p. 18). Accordingly, sexual assaults that are perpetrated by a coworker or in the workplace are likely to also be classified as sexual harassment. Indeed, based on data from the 2014 RMWS survey, among service members who were sexually assaulted in the past year, 49 percent indicated that the assault occurred during duty hours, 43 percent indicated that the assault took place "at work," and the vast majority indicated that the offender(s) included a service member or a civilian or contractor working for the military (95 percent) (Jaycox et al., 2015). Given that, in many cases, the same incident can be categorized as sexual harassment and sexual assault, the two measures will be positively correlated.

Second, individual characteristics that increase risk for sexual harassment victimization may simultaneously increase risk for sexual assault victimization. Service members who are young, female, unmarried, enlisted, lower ranked, not in the Air Force, or assigned to a workplace with a gender ratio that tilts toward men are at increased risk for sexual harassment (Buchanan, Settles, and Woods, 2008; Defense Manpower Data

Center, 2011; Defense Manpower Data Center, 2013; Farris et al., 2015; Fitzgerald et al., 1997; Harned et al., 2002; LeardMann et al., 2013; Schell and Morral, 2015a; Schell and Morral, 2015b; Schell et al., forthcoming; Street et al., 2007) and for sexual assault (Harned et al., 2002; Jaycox et al., 2015; Kimerling et al., 2007; LeardMann et al., 2013; Sadler et al., 2003; Schell and Morral, 2015a; Schell et al., forthcoming; Street et al., 2016; Street et al., 2008). It may be that the observed relationship between sexual harassment and sexual assault can be explained, in part, by these types of factors that increase service members' risk of both.

Alternatively, there could be characteristics of the workplace that increase risk of both sexual harassment and sexual assault (the third possible explanation). Candidate workplace risk factors might include weak oversight or leadership, breakdowns in good order and discipline, and a permissive attitude toward demeaning or abusive behavior. In such environments, employees may come to a shared expectation that sexual harassment is tolerated and even expected. It could be that, as workers listen to sexual joking, watch as coworkers romantically or sexually proposition others in the workplace, or hear rumors of inappropriate touching, they learn with each instance whether these behaviors are likely to be socially or professionally penalized. For individuals with a propensity to engage in sexual harassment, these learning opportunities provide insight into the likelihood that they too would escape social and professional sanctions. In turn, as workers learn that their harassing behaviors are accepted by those in their professional environment, there is less reason to inhibit decisions to engage in more-extreme behaviors that eventually pass the threshold to sexual assault. Consistent with this hypothesis, the DoD *2014–2016 Sexual Assault Prevention Strategy* suggests that a "unit or command where women are objectified or demeaned or inappropriate comments about race or sexual orientation go uncorrected" may create the impression that service members "may get away with other acts against women or men, including sexual assault" (DoD, 2014, p. 6). Sadler et al., 2003, reports that women who had observed their ranking officer allowing others in the unit to make sexually demeaning comments were more likely to have been sexually assaulted during their military service.

To explore whether there is other supportive evidence for this third (environmental) explanation of the relationship between sexual harassment and sexual assault risk, we pursued an analytic strategy that was designed to control for the first and second explanations. This allowed us to determine whether, and to what degree, the relationship between sexual harassment and sexual assault persists after accounting for definitional overlap and shared risk factors for the two events. To do so, we assessed the relationship between ambient sexual harassment and sexual assault. *Ambient* sexual harassment refers to the percentage of colleagues in the workplace who are sexually harassed; the percentage does not include any sexual harassment that the individual experiences (Glomb et al., 1997). This approach eliminates inflation of the relationship that occurs when a single workplace event is counted as both sexual harassment and sexual assault. It also ensures that the individual's risk factors contribute to only one estimate (sexual assault) but not the other (ambient sexual harassment), which, in turn, eliminates the correlation caused by most shared individual risk factors.

Ambient sexual harassment was first defined and studied in civilian work groups (Schneider, 1996). Working in civilian environments where others are sexually harassed has been found to reduce job satisfaction, which, in turn, increases job withdrawal (e.g., intentions to quit) among both female employees (Glomb et al., 1997) and male employees (Richman-Hirsch and Glomb, 2002). In addition, team cohesion declines in work groups with higher levels of ambient sexual hostility (i.e., insulting sexual verbal and nonverbal behaviors) (Raver and Gelfand, 2005). Researchers have suggested that exposure to sexual harassment against others may stress workers who feel guilty about not being able to protect their coworkers from harassment, who worry about being sexually harassed themselves, and who feel angry with their organization for an ineffective response (Glomb et al., 1997). The published work on ambient sexual harassment in civilian workplaces suggests a negative effect on worker satisfaction and team performance, although most of this work has been done on relatively small samples of workers and may have limited generalizability. Although one study that found a strong association between an individual's perception of sexual harassment in his or her environment and their own risk of sexual assault (Harris, 2007), this study could not rule out the possibility that individual characteristics or certain methodological artifacts accounted for the association. In a subsequent study using an analytic strategy that controlled for individual characteristics, Harris, McDonald, and Sparks, 2018, reported that ambient sexism in the military work environment increased risk of sexual harassment. However, to our knowledge, the study reported here is the first to examine ambient sexual harassment on risk for more-extreme violence, such as sexual assault.

In the next chapter, we describe the data and procedures that we used to construct ambient sexual harassment scores for each RMWS respondent, by gender, and how we evaluated the association of these scores with each individual's sexual assault risk. In Chapter Three, we present findings from these analyses. And in Chapter Four, we take up the implications of the analyses, along with recommendations for how this report's findings might be used to improve efforts to prevent sexual assault and possibly other unwanted workplace behaviors, such as sexual harassment.

CHAPTER TWO

Data and Methods

This chapter describes the data that we used to understand the relationship between ambient sexual harassment and sexual assault, as well as our statistical methods. In brief, we developed measures of ambient sexual harassment of service men and women using survey data on unwanted workplace experiences collected through the 2014 RMWS. The ambient sexual harassment of approximately 115,000 service members was based only on the experiences of the people they worked with (in the same unit, installation, or major command), not on their own experiences. For example, if a high percentage of an individual's female colleagues reported experiences meeting DoD definitions of sexual harassment, then that individual's score for ambient sexual harassment of women would be correspondingly high. Similarly, if a high percentage of men in the individual's work environment were sexually harassed, then his or her score for ambient sexual harassment of men would be high. We then used regression models to examine how ambient sexual harassment predicts each individual's sexual assault risk, over and above other known risk factors for sexual assault.

Data

In 2014, DoD asked the RAND Corporation to conduct an independent assessment of sexual assault, sexual harassment, and gender discrimination in the military. The RMWS was one of the largest surveys of its kind: Almost 560,000 active- and reserve-component service members were invited to participate in this representatively sampled survey, and more than 170,000 completed the web-administered survey questions. Although the RMWS includes a small number of respondents from the reserve component and from the Coast Guard, the present analyses focus exclusively on results from the active component of the four DoD services (Army, Navy, Air Force, Marine Corps). Details of the overall study design can be found in Volume 1 of this report series (Morral, Gore, and Schell, 2014).

Members of the active component were randomized to receive either the new RMWS measures of sexual assault and harassment (*the RAND form*) or the measures previously used to assess these constructs (*the prior form*); at the time, the prior form had last been used by DoD in the 2012 Workplace and Gender Relations Survey of Active Duty Members. Separate sample weights were constructed for each form to make responses representative of the sample frame of all 1.3 million active-component service members below the rank of general or flag officers. The data analyzed here are from the 115,759 service members who completed the RAND form assessing sexual harassment and sexual assault experiences.

For the RMWS survey, RAND newly designed measures of sexual assault and sexual harassment to align more closely with the Uniform Code of Military Justice crimes of unwanted sexual contact and to the DoD definition of sexual harassment found in DoD Directive 1350.2. The survey included behaviorally specific screening items, which, when endorsed, were followed by questions ascertaining whether each of the legal criteria for establishing the presence of either a sexual assault or sexual harassment were met. For instance, the first two (of six) screening items for sexual assault were as follows:

1. Since [date one year prior to survey administration], did you have any unwanted experiences in which someone put his penis into your [if female, then display "vagina,"] anus or mouth?
2. Since [date one year prior to survey administration], did you have any *unwanted* experiences in which someone put any object or any body part *other than a penis* into your [if female, then display "vagina,"] anus or mouth? The body part could include a finger, tongue or testicles.

Respondents who endorsed either of these screening items were next asked questions to establish whether force or coercion had been used or attempted during the unwanted contact, as well as whether the respondent believed that the unwanted contact sought to achieve a sexual purpose or to humiliate or abuse the respondent. Respondents who experienced one of the screening items, indicated that the experience involved some kind of force, and indicated that it was for a sexual purpose or to humiliate or abuse them met each of the criteria for having experienced a past-year sexual assault; thus, such respondents were counted for survey purposes as having experienced a sexual assault in the past year. For the complete survey instrument and information on its development, see Morral, Gore, and Schell, 2014. RMWS survey results indicated that, across DoD service branches, the estimated percentage of service members who experienced a past-year sexual assault was 4.87 percent (confidence interval [CI]: 4.61–5.14) for women and 0.95 percent (CI: 0.78–1.15) for men (Morral, Gore, and Schell, 2015).

Similarly, sexual harassment was established using a set of 13 behavioral screener items on upsetting or offensive workplace experiences, which were followed by questions establishing whether (1) any such experience continued despite the coworker knowing that the respondent was upset by it and (2) it was sufficiently offensive that most members of the military would have been offended by it. Individuals who endorsed a screener item and either of the follow-up questions were treated for survey purposes as having experienced sexual harassment in the past year. RMWS survey results indicated that, across DoD service branches, the estimated percentage of service members who experienced past-year sexual harassment was 21.57 percent (CI: 20.96–22.19) for women and 6.61 percent (CI: 6.09–7.15) for men (National Defense Research Institute, 2014).

Survey nonresponse was accounted for using nonresponse weighting. Details of these weights are described in Morral, Gore, and Schell, 2014, and assessments of nonresponse bias after weighting are provided in Morral, Gore, and Schell, 2016. Because of the nonresponse weighting, we have no need to impute missing values resulting from survey nonresponse. However, an additional form of missingness resulted from the planned missingness design used in the RMWS study. The RMWS design randomly varied the questionnaire form that service members received. Some service members ($n = 66,419$) received the full sexual harassment module, which included 13 inappropriate workplace behavior screening items and the follow-up questions designed to establish whether endorsed screening items met all legal criteria for sexual harassment. Other service members ($n = 49,340$) were randomly assigned to complete a shorter form of the survey, which included the 13 sexual harassment screening items but not the additional follow-up items needed to establish whether any inappropriate workplace behaviors constituted sexual harassment. For these respondents to the shorter form, we used an imputation strategy to account for the missing data. Because every respondent got the key screening questions about various upsetting sexual behaviors by coworkers, the only imputation was whether the upsetting sexual behavior was serious enough to qualify as sexual harassment.

The majority of the item nonresponse that affects the calculation of the sexual harassment measure was due to the planned missingness design, which randomly selected respondents to receive only the sexual harassment screening items, not the full sexual harassment module. Of 115,137.8 person-years over which ambient sexual harassment can be calculated for survey respondents, 51,631.2 had missing values on the sexual harassment measure because of either item nonresponse or planned missingness. Planned missingness accounted for 98 percent of the missing values among survey respondents (49,075).

Because these data were missing completely at random, (1) excluding missing values from the analysis would not yield any bias, (2) simple mean imputation for missing values would not yield any bias, and (3) individual service member characteristics were unrelated to the missingness by design. In this case, however, we could impute values much more precisely than using simple means yet still use the planned missingness design to ensure that the results were unbiased.

Specifically, because all respondents completed the 13 sexual harassment screening items, some respondents could be logically imputed as having experienced or not experienced sexual harassment without error. In particular,

- Of the 49,947.8 person-years with missing sexual harassment information, 771.1 person-years were logically imputed as including a sexual harassment, because the respondents endorsed items that automatically qualify as sexual harassment, without the need for additional follow-up questions. (For example, item SH10: "Since [Date], did someone from work intentionally touch you in a sexual way when you did not want them to? This could include touching your genitals, breasts, buttocks, or touching you with their genitals anywhere on your body.")
- Similarly, survey respondents who responded negatively to all of the sexual harassment screening questions were logically imputed as not experiencing sexual harassment (42,025.6 person-years).

These two logical imputations account for more than 86 percent of the missing sexual harassment data and correspond to imputations that were without error. The remaining 14 percent of missing sexual harassment data were imputed with a logistic regression predicting past-year sexual harassment among respondents who completed the full sexual harassment module and who indicated experiencing at least one of the screening item behaviors, using as predictors all the screening items (except for the sexual touching item used in the logical imputation). Predicted values from this model served as imputed sexual harassment risk probabilities for short-form respondents who had not had their past-year sexual harassment value logically imputed. Imputations from this model were restricted to a sample that endorsed at least one of the screener items and, therefore, had a higher predicted prevalence of sexual harassment (68.1 percent, on average). The average predicted value weighted by person-months for those who experienced past-year sexual harassment was 73.6 percent, while the average for those who did not was 56.5 percent. As noted earlier, the performance of this imputation model did not introduce bias in our estimates. It served only as a way to improve the precision of our ambient sexual harassment measure.

Defining Ambient Sexual Harassment

Part of the reason that sexual harassment and sexual assault are highly correlated at the individual level is because many incidents of sexual assault also qualify as sexual harassment. To avoid conflating an individual service member's ambient sexual harassment exposure with his or her personal sexual harassment victimization experiences, we defined a service member's *ambient sexual harassment* as the annual rate of sexual harassment against colleagues in the same environment, excluding that particular service member (Glomb et al., 1997).

For each service member, we initially derived six ambient sexual harassment estimates that varied gender of colleagues (sexual harassment against men or women) by three levels of the service member's environment (unit, installation, and major command). We measured ambient sexual harassment against male and female colleagues separately because we had no *a priori* belief that ambient sexual harassment against women and ambient sexual harassment against men have the same relationship with sexual assault risk.

The rate of ambient sexual harassment was developed using three levels of a service member's environment: unit (based on each member's assigned unit identification code), installation (based on postal code of the duty unit as a proxy), and major command (based on the major command code for service members in the Army, Navy, and Air Force, or the monitored command code for service members in the Marine Corps). At each level, we calculated the weighted percentage of male and female service members (excluding the individual) who were sexually harassed in the past year (i.e., fiscal year 2014). Our final measure of a service member's exposure to ambient sexual harassment was a simple average of the percentage of colleagues who were sexually harassed at each of the three levels of the individual's work environment.

Smoothing Noise from Small Work Environments

After imputation, ambient sexual harassment estimates at the unit, installation, and major command levels were adjusted to reduce sampling variability associated with especially small aggregations of service members. Specifically, military environments that have few service members or where few members completed the RMWS survey are much more likely to have extreme values on measures of ambient harassment (see Table 2.1 for the size distribution of each environment). For example, consider a unit that has only two women working at it, one of whom was sexually harassed in the past year. The ambient sexual harassment estimate for the woman who was harassed

Table 2.1
Person-Year Size Distribution of Units, Installations, and Major Commands, by the Number of RMWS Respondents of Each Gender

Gender	Cluster Type	Number of Clusters with N RMWS Respondents		
		$N < 10$	$10 \leq N < 24$	$N \geq 24$
Women	Unit	27,463.8	15,966.0	11,621.1
	Installation	1,933.1	1,519.0	51,598.8
	Major command	364.8	663.3	54,022.8
Men	Unit	33,963.0	18,618.0	11,478.2
	Installation	2,753.3	1,942.7	59,363.2
	Major command	400.4	798.3	62,860.4

is 0 (or 0 percent) because all of the other women in her unit (one woman) were not harassed. The ambient sexual harassment estimate for the woman who was not harassed is 1 (or 100 percent) because all of the other women in her unit (one) were harassed. But 0 and 1 are clearly poor estimates of the true ambient risk to which each woman was exposed. To avoid these extreme values in small samples, we smoothed the ambient sexual harassment estimates toward the overall service-by-gender rates of ambient sexual harassment. This technique is sometimes called additive smoothing, Laplace smoothing, or Bayesian averaging. In the example described here, for instance, the woman who was not harassed would have an ambient sexual harassment score constructed as though there were an additional K other women in the unit whose exposure to harassment occurred at the rate observed for all women across the service branch. We determined the optimal level of smoothing by choosing the number of such pseudo-observations at the service-gender level to add into each environment that maximized the association of ambient sexual harassment and sexual assault risk. The value that achieved this maximum was $K = 24$. Statistical details for this procedure are provided in the appendix.

Specifically, for each gender, we added to each unit 24 pseudo-observations with sexual harassment at the service-gender prevalence. Then, for each service member, we calculated the prevalence of sexual harassment among men and women for each unit, excluding that particular service member. Note that service members changed units throughout the study period, so we applied this process for each of the 12 months under study and then calculated the average for each service member, weighted by the time the individual spent in each setting. Finally, we averaged the six measures of ambient sexual harassment prevalence (two genders by three organizational levels) to constitute our measure of the service member's exposure to ambient sexual harassment.

Analytic Strategy

To explore the relationship between ambient sexual harassment and sexual assault risk, we fit weighted logistic regression models. Let SH_i^f and SH_i^m denote ambient sexual harassment against women and men at the optimal smoothing level. The most general model is described here, but all other models are simplifications of this same model. Consider the following weighted logistic regression separately for each gender:

$$\text{logit}(\Pr(SA_i = 1)) = \beta_0 + \beta_1 SH_i^m + \beta_2 SH_i^f + \beta_3 X_i,$$

where X_i is the following set of service member characteristics or risk factors:

- gender (male, female)
- date of birth

- race/ethnicity (Asian, black, Hispanic, white, other)
- pre-service sexual assault[1]
- marital status (single, married)
- total number of dependents
- education (high school or less, some college, college degree, graduate degree, missing)
- Armed Forces Qualification Test score
- service branch (Army, Navy, Air Force, Marine Corps)
- pay grade (E1–E3, E4, E5–E6, E7–E9, O1–O3, O4–O6, W1–W5)
- years of active federal service by pay grade category (interaction term)
- military accession type/source of commission (enlisted, Reserve Officers' Training Corps, officer academy, other)
- months deployed since September 11, 2001
- DoD occupational group (20 categories, ten each for enlisted and officers).[2]

The coefficients β_1 and β_2 represent the log-odds ratio of sexual assault risk for a unit change in ambient sexual harassment. Although these log-odds ratios are useful in determining the direction and magnitude of the relationship, they are more challenging to interpret than either a risk difference or a risk ratio is. To clarify their interpretation, we used a recycled prediction approach to estimate the marginal effects at the average ambient sexual harassment level among service members who were exposed to above-average ambient sexual harassment compared with the average ambient sexual harassment level among service members who were exposed to below-average ambient sexual harassment. In this approach, we estimated the expected sexual assault risk if all service members were exposed to a particular level of ambient sexual harassment by averaging the individual service member's predicted sexual assault risk with ambient sexual harassment set at that value.

To explore service differences, we fit similar models that included interactions between service and ambient sexual harassment. Once we determined a final model, we estimated service-specific risk differences and risk ratio using the recycled prediction approach within each service.

---

[1] Pre-service sexual assault is a measure indicating whether the member had been sexually assaulted before entering the military (by self-report). It was measured with question SAFU40 on the RMWS survey (see Morral, Gore, and Schell, 2014, Appendix A).

[2] For additional information on the association between the factors in this list and sexual assault and sexual harassment, see Schell et al., forthcoming.

CHAPTER THREE

Ambient Sexual Harassment and Sexual Assault Risk

In this chapter, we describe the distribution of ambient sexual harassment against women and men and the association between ambient sexual harassment and sexual assault risk. Specifically, we compare how service members' risk of sexual assault would be expected to change if they moved from an environment characterized by a typically low rate of ambient sexual harassment (the average ambient sexual harassment rate for members serving in environments with rates below the average DoD or service rate of ambient sexual harassment) to an environment with a typically high rate (the average ambient sexual harassment rate for those serving in environments with rates above average DoD or service rates), and we compare how these associations vary by service branch.

Exposure to Ambient Sexual Harassment

Table 3.1 provides descriptive statistics on the distribution of ambient sexual harassment by gender of the individual and the gender of colleagues who were sexually harassed. Results from the RMWS survey indicate that, on average, service women worked in environments where 20 percent of their female colleagues and 6 percent of their male colleagues had been sexually harassed in the past year. On average, service

Table 3.1
Average Exposure to Ambient Sexual Harassment Against Men and Women in the Military, by Gender of the Service Member

Gender of the Service Member	Ambient Sexual Harassment Against	Mean	Standard Deviation	Minimum	Maximum
Woman	Service women	0.20	0.063	0.07	0.41
	Service men	0.06	0.020	0.02	0.17
Man	Service women	0.22	0.059	0.08	0.41
	Service men	0.06	0.018	0.02	0.17

men worked in environments where 22 percent of their female colleagues and 6 percent of their male colleagues had been sexually harassed in the past year. The slight difference in the rates of ambient sexual harassment against the female colleagues of women and the female colleagues of men (for example) may reflect slight differences, on average, in the population of women who worked with other women compared with women who worked with men. For instance, if some women worked in small units composed exclusively of women, then the population of women serving with men did not include the experiences of all women in the military. The same would be true if some men worked in small units that included only men.

The DoD-wide means for ambient sexual harassment against men and women were necessarily very close to DoD estimates of the proportion of men and women in the services who were exposed to sexual harassment over the same period (21.4 percent for women, 6.6 percent for men) (Farris et al., 2015). However, the large standard deviations and minimum and maximum ranges for ambient sexual harassment indicate that some service members were exposed to substantially more or less ambient sexual harassment than others. For instance, women serving in environments that were one standard deviation below the average for ambient sexual harassment of women experienced approximately half the ambient sexual harassment of women as those serving in environments that were one standard deviation above the mean. Indeed, at the extremes, some members served in a unit, installation, and major command where an average of 7 percent of women were sexually harassed, while others served where 41 percent of women were sexually harassed. For men, the range spanned an eightfold difference: Some members served in units, installations, and major commands where just 2 percent of their male peers were sexually harassed, while others served where 17 percent of men were sexually harassed.

Table 3.2 provides summary statistics of ambient sexual harassment by service. A large portion of the variability in ambient sexual harassment occurred across service branches rather than within them. Airmen were exposed to the lowest mean levels of ambient sexual harassment against women and men. Marines were exposed to the highest mean levels of ambient sexual harassment against women, and sailors and solders were exposed to the highest mean level of ambient sexual harassment against men. In the Navy, clusters of service members were exposed to particularly high levels of ambient sexual harassment against women and men (as illustrated by the hashmarks at the extreme of the distributions in Figures 3.1 and 3.2). Whereas the airmen with the highest rates of ambient sexual harassment served in units, installations, and major commands where around 6 percent of men and 20 percent of women were harassed, some sailors served in environments where rates were more than twice as high. These highest-risk environments may include some ships: A separate analysis found ships to be among the installations with the highest rates of sexual harassment across services (Morral et al., 2018).

Table 3.2
Average Exposure to Ambient Sexual Harassment Against Men and Women in the Military, by Service

Service	Ambient Sexual Harassment Against	Mean	Standard Deviation	Minimum	Maximum
Army	Service women	0.22	0.022	0.13	0.29
	Service men	0.07	0.009	0.03	0.11
Navy	Service women	0.26	0.043	0.14	0.41
	Service men	0.07	0.017	0.03	0.17
Air Force	Service women	0.12	0.016	0.07	0.20
	Service men	0.03	0.006	0.02	0.06
Marine Corps	Service women	0.27	0.024	0.16	0.35
	Service men	0.06	0.010	0.02	0.09

Figure 3.1
Distribution of Ambient Sexual Harassment Against Women, by Service

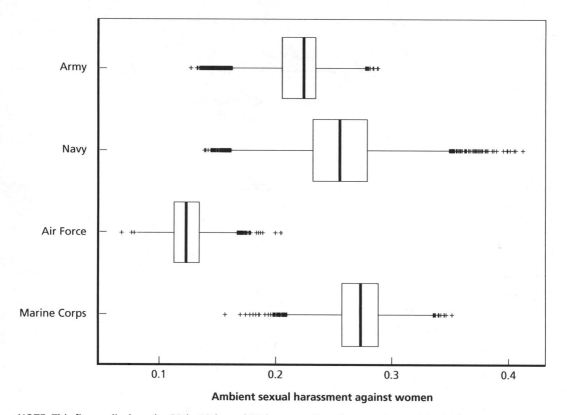

Ambient sexual harassment against women

NOTE: This figure displays the 25th, 50th, and 75th percentile values as a box, with whiskers extending 1.5 times the length of the interquartile range from the edge of the box. Values that are more extreme than the whiskers are plotted individually with the "+" symbol.

Figure 3.2
Distribution of Ambient Sexual Harassment Against Men, by Service

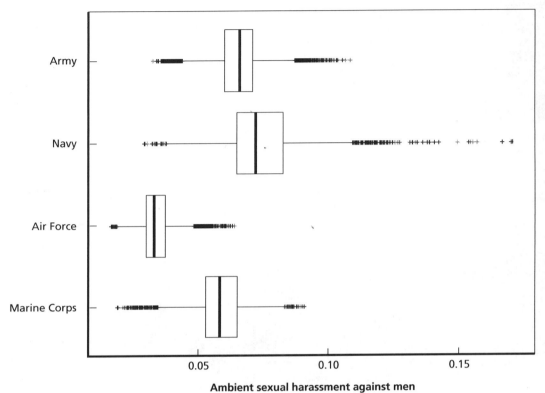

NOTE: This figure displays the 25th, 50th, and 75th percentile values as a box, with whiskers extending 1.5 times the length of the interquartile range from the edge of the box. Values that are more extreme than the whiskers are plotted individually with the "+" symbol.

Relationship Between Ambient Sexual Harassment and Sexual Assault Risk

Bivariate associations between ambient sexual harassment and sexual assault risk are provided in Table 3.3. We compared (1) the average sexual assault risk faced by a service member working in an environment with a typically low rate of ambient sexual harassment (i.e., the average ambient sexual harassment rate among environments below average for ambient sexual harassment across DoD) and (2) the average sexual assault risk faced by a service member working in an environment with a typically high rate of ambient sexual harassment (i.e., the average ambient sexual harassment rate among environments above average for ambient sexual harassment across DoD). The risk differences and risk ratios in Table 3.3 compare sexual assault risk among service members exposed to typically high and low rates of ambient sexual harassment. For example, the unadjusted risk difference in the first row of Table 3.3 shows

Table 3.3
Unadjusted and Adjusted Bivariate Relationship Between Ambient Sexual Harassment and Sexual Assault Risk Comparing Service Members Serving in Environments with Above- or Below-Average Rates of Ambient Sexual Harassment

Gender of the Service Member	Ambient Sexual Harassment Against	Unadjusted			Adjusted		
		Risk Difference (95% CI)	Risk Ratio (95% CI)	p-value	Risk Difference (95% CI)	Risk Ratio (95% CI)	p-value
Woman	Service women	0.032 (0.027–0.036)	2.07 (1.88–2.28)	<0.001	0.023 (0.013–0.032)	1.66 (1.33–2.08)	<0.001
	Service men	0.026 (0.022–0.031)	1.81 (1.65–1.98)	<0.001	0.020 (0.014–0.027)	1.57 (1.34–1.84)	<0.001
Man	Service women	0.007 (0.005–0.010)	2.68 (1.98–3.63)	<0.001	0.005 (0.001–0.009)	1.88 (1.10–3.22)	0.018
	Service men	0.007 (0.005–0.009)	2.31 (1.79–2.98)	<0.001	0.005 (0.002–0.007)	1.79 (1.25–2.55)	0.001

NOTE: Risk differences and risk ratios compare (1) the sexual assault risk of service members serving in environments with above-average rates of ambient sexual harassment and (2) the sexual assault risk of those serving in environments with below-average rates of ambient sexual harassment. Adjusted estimates control for the risk factors identified in Chapter Two.

that an additional 3.2 percent of women working in environments with above-average rates of ambient sexual harassment against women were sexually assaulted relative to women working in environments with below-average rates of ambient sexual harassment against women. The same pattern can be described with the risk ratio, which is interpreted as indicating that service women working in environments with above-average ambient sexual harassment against women were 2.07 times more likely to be sexually assaulted in that year as were service women working in environments with below-average ambient sexual harassment against women. These unadjusted risk ratios were all above 1.8 for men and women, indicating that the sexual assault risk for service members in an environment with above-average ambient sexual harassment was nearly double the sexual assault risk of those in environments with below-average ambient sexual harassment.

After we controlled for all the other risk factors of sexual assault (such as date of birth and pay grade; see the full list identified in Chapter Two), all risk differences and risk ratios were attenuated but remained large and statistically significant. For instance, women serving in environments with above-average ambient sexual harassment of women had 1.66 times the risk of sexual assault as did women serving in environments with below-average risk of ambient sexual harassment of women. The risk of sexual assault against men was 1.79 times higher when men served in environments with above-average ambient sexual harassment of men.

The sexual assault risk for both women and men seems to be about equally associated with the presence of ambient harassment of men and ambient harassment of women. This could occur because the ambient harassment of women is highly correlated with the ambient harassment of men or because the ambient harassment of men and of women each contributes independently to service members' sexual assault risk. To evaluate these alternative explanations, we examined members' sexual assault risk as a function of both ambient harassment of women and ambient harassment of men after accounting for all of the risk factors identified in Chapter Two.

In Table 3.4, conditional risk differences and risk ratios show the results from comparing (1) the expected sexual assault risk if all service members experienced above-average ambient sexual harassment against women (or men) and (2) the expected sexual assault risk if all service members experienced below-average ambient sexual harassment against women (or men), while holding ambient sexual harassment against the other gender constant. For instance, women in environments with above-average ambient sexual harassment of women had 1.30 times the sexual assault risk as women in environments with below-average ambient harassment of women, holding ambient sexual harassment of men constant. Women's risk of sexual assault appears to be sensitive to the amount of ambient sexual harassment of men. Whereas moving from an environment with below-average ambient harassment of women to one with above-average

Table 3.4
Adjusted Multivariate Relationship Between Ambient Sexual Harassment and Sexual Assault Risk Comparing Service Members Serving in Environments with Above or Below Average Rates of Sexual Harassment

Gender of the Service Member	Ambient Sexual Harassment Against	Conditional Risk Difference (95% CI)	Conditional Risk Ratio (95% CI)	p-value	Marginal Risk Difference (95% CI)	Marginal Risk Ratio (95% CI)
Woman	Service women	0.012 (0.001–0.023)	1.30 (1.01–1.68)	0.042	0.028 (0.018–0.037)	1.88 (1.50–2.35)
	Service men	0.016 (0.008–0.024)	1.44 (1.19–1.73)	<0.001		
Man	Service women	0.002 (−0.003–0.008)	1.31 (0.64–2.69)	0.457	0.006 (0.003–0.010)	2.20 (1.34–3.62)
	Service men	0.004 (0.001–0.008)	1.67 (1.04–2.68)	0.033		

NOTE: Conditional risk differences and ratios compare (1) the expected sexual assault risk if all service members served in environments with above-average rates of ambient sexual harassment of one gender and (2) the expected sexual assault risk if all service members served in environments with below-average rates of ambient sexual harassment of the same gender, holding constant the rate of ambient sexual harassment of the other gender. Marginal risk differences and ratios compare (1) the sexual assault risk of members serving in environments with above-average rates of ambient sexual harassment against men and women and (2) the sexual assault risk of members serving in environments with below-average rates of ambient sexual harassment against men and women. All estimates control for the risk factors identified in Chapter Two.

ambient harassment of women was associated with a 1.2-percentage-point increase in women's sexual assault risk, moving from an environment with below-average to above-average ambient harassment of men increased a woman's sexual assault risk by 1.6 percentage points.

The marginal risk differences and risk ratios reported in Table 3.4 show how the sexual assault risk would be different (1) if the rates of ambient harassment of men and the ambient harassment of women were both above average and (2) if the rates were both below average. These marginal risk ratios were both greater than 1.8. The sexual assault risk of a female service member was 1.88 times higher in an environment that had above-average ambient sexual harassment against men and women than the sexual assault risk in an environment with below-average ambient sexual harassment against both genders. Similarly, service men's risk of sexual assault was 2.20 times higher in an environment with above-average ambient sexual harassment of both genders than the risk of sexual assault in an environment with below-average ambient harassment of both genders. Together, these results suggest that ambient harassment of women and ambient harassment of men are correlated but also independently contribute to the sexual assault risk faced by men and women in the services.

Service Differences in the Relationship Between Ambient Sexual Harassment and Sexual Assault Risk

After establishing the relationship between ambient sexual harassment and sexual assault risk, we assessed whether that relationship varied across services. Table 3.5 provides estimates of the relationship between ambient sexual harassment and individual sexual assault risk within each service branch. To describe these relationships, we compare sexual assault risk between individuals in environments where the rates of ambient sexual harassment against both women and men are above average versus the risk for individuals working where both rates are below average. To simplify, this table combines the male and female ambient harassment effects and presents the joint effect associated with serving in an environment where the rates of ambient harassment against both women and men are below average versus serving where the rates are above average. For women, there was a significant interaction between service branch and the effect of serving in a below-average versus above-average ambient sexual harassment environment on sexual assault risk. A shift in ambient sexual harassment of men and women from the average below-average rate to the average above-average rate was associated with an increase of sexual assault risk by a factor of between 1.21 and 1.62 in each service other than the Marine Corps, where ambient sexual harassment did not appear to be significantly associated with sexual assault risk.

For men, there was also a significant interaction between service branch and the effect of ambient sexual harassment on sexual assault risk. Service-specific effects were

Table 3.5
Sexual Assault Risk Differences and Ratios for Service Members in Environments with Above-Average Versus Below-Average Ambient Sexual Harassment of Women and Men

	Risk Difference (95% CI)	Risk Ratio (95% CI)
Sexual assault risk for women		
Army	0.011 (0.004–0.019)	1.29 (1.09–1.52)
Navy	0.031 (0.019–0.042)	1.62 (1.36–1.94)
Air Force	0.006 (0.002–0.011)	1.21 (1.01–1.45)
Marine Corps	0.004 (−0.018–0.026)	1.05 (0.79–1.39)
Sexual assault risk for men		
Army	0.000 (−0.004–0.005)	1.03 (0.65–1.62)
Navy	0.009 (0.004–0.014)	1.98 (1.45–2.70)
Air Force	−0.002 (−0.004–0.000)	0.52 (0.22–1.23)
Marine Corps	0.002 (−0.003–0.007)	1.26 (0.68–2.31)

significant only in the Navy, where an increase from the average below-average rates of ambient sexual harassment to the average above-average rates was associated with a doubling of men's risk of sexual assault. However, these within-service effect sizes among men should be interpreted cautiously because they have considerably less precision than the other estimates we have presented. This occurs because, within any individual service, there were few male sexual assault victims in the survey sample, and the range of the ambient sexual harassment within each service was much narrower than when looking across DoD. Because of these factors, when looking at the association among men and within services, we cannot provide very reliable estimates. In the current study, we did not find significant effects when looking at male sexual assault risk within the Army, Air Force, or Marine Corps; however, we did not have sufficient statistical power to expect to find such effects, even if they existed.

Ambient Sexual Harassment Improves the Prediction of Sexual Assault Risk

The risk factors identified in Chapter Two (e.g., date of birth, race/ethnicity, marital status, pay grade) are relatively good predictors of sexual assault risk. These variables alone explain a fair amount of the variance in an individual's sexual assault risk. In an earlier report, we found that a model of sexual assault risk using these variables had a Tjur's R^2 equal to 0.0670 (or 6.70 percentage points) for women and 0.0327 (or 3.27 percentage points) for men (Schell et al., forthcoming, pp. 31, 39). Tjur's R^2 can be interpreted here as indicating how effectively the entire regression model differentiates the risks of those who were sexually assaulted from those who were not. Specifically, a model of sexual assault risk using just the risk factors identified in Chapter Two can be used to predict that the average past-year sexual assault risk to women who were not assaulted in the past year was 4.5 percent, whereas the average risk among those who were assaulted was 11.2 percent. Similarly, men who were not assaulted in the past year would be predicted to have a risk of 0.9 percent, whereas those who were assaulted would be predicted to have more than four times higher risk (4.2 percent) (Schell et al., forthcoming). Adding information about ambient sexual assault to these models improves their prediction of sexual assault risk nontrivially (Tjur's R^2 increases to 0.071 for women and 0.037 for men).

Ambient sexual harassment also improves the prediction of sexual assault risk in models that include many additional risk factors, including other features of service members' work environments. For instance, in the same earlier study, we examined models of sexual assault risk that included all of the risk factors identified in Chapter Two, as well as factors indicating whether the member was deployed during the past year; served on a ship; left the service in the past year; or served in units, installations, or commands where there were large numbers of people, large proportions of men, younger service members, and other characteristics (Schell et al., forthcoming). The most powerful such model we evaluated had Tjur's R^2 values of 0.072 for women and 0.045 for men. When we add information about ambient sexual harassment, the values increase to 0.073 and 0.048, respectively. This represents a small but nontrivial improvement in the prediction of women's sexual assault risk and a relatively large improvement in the prediction of men's risk. For comparison, of the 30 factors included in the risk model that excludes ambient harassment information, only three factors improved the prediction of men's sexual assault risk by as much or more than ambient sexual harassment does. These factors were pre-service sexual assault, occupational group, and separation from the military in the past year.

Summary

The rates of ambient sexual harassment varied substantially at the units, installations, and major commands in which members of the military serve. In some environments, only 7 percent of service women were sexually harassed; in other environments, the rate was six times higher. Ambient sexual harassment of men spanned from 2 percent to 17 percent, an eightfold difference in risk.

Ambient sexual harassment against women and men was strongly associated with risk of sexual assault, even after controlling for many other sexual assault risk factors (those identified in Chapter Two). Indeed, women's sexual assault risk increased by more than a factor of 1.5 when they worked in environments with above-average rates of ambient sexual harassment against women or men, compared with the sexual assault risk for women working where the rates were below the DoD average. Men's risk of sexual assault increased by a factor of 1.8 in such environments.

The association between ambient sexual harassment and sexual assault risk differed for women and men in each branch of service. Women serving in the Navy had, on average, the highest associations between ambient sexual harassment and sexual assault, whereas those in the Air Force had the lowest association, and these associations were significant for each service other than the Marine Corps. For men, however, a significant association was found only in the Navy, where it was quite strong: Navy men serving in environments with above-average ambient sexual harassment rates had 2.0 times the risk of being sexually assaulted as Navy men serving where the rates were below average.

The association between ambient sexual harassment and sexual assault risk is not explained by other known risk factors for sexual assault that we or others have examined. In addition, it makes a unique contribution to explaining sexual assault risk over and above the most-powerful models of sexual assault risk that we previously developed (see Schell et al., forthcoming). It makes a small improvement in the models' prediction of women's sexual assault risk and quite substantial improvements in the prediction of men's sexual assault risk.

CHAPTER FOUR

Conclusion

The observed relationship between sexual harassment and sexual assault in the military has a few plausible explanations, as described in Chapter One. First, it may be an artifact of definitional overlap; that is, some sexual harassment incidents are so severe that they are also sexual assaults. Second, both sexual harassment and sexual assault share many risk factors (e.g., younger age, workplaces with a higher proportion of male workers); these common risk factors may explain the observed correlation between sexual harassment and sexual assault. In this report, we used an analytic strategy that ruled out definitional overlap as an explanation for the high correlation between sexual assault and sexual harassment, and we accounted for a large number of known shared risk factors. Nevertheless, strong positive associations remained between sexual assault and sexual harassment.

To rule out definitional overlap and the contribution of shared risk factors to the relationship between sexual harassment and sexual assault, we first created *ambient* sexual harassment rates for each service member. These rates summarize the percentage of the individual's colleagues at the unit, installation, and major command levels who were sexually harassed during the past year. By exploring the link between ambient sexual harassment—instead of personal sexual harassment—and the individual service member's sexual assault risk, we can be more certain that (1) a spurious association is not created by double-counting a single incident as both harassment and assault and (2) the association between ambient harassment and sexual assault risk is unlikely to have been created by unmeasured individual risk factors, because ambient harassment for each individual was assessed using data from other individuals.

Our analyses revealed that the relationship between ambient sexual harassment in the work environment and an individual's risk of being sexually assaulted is robust. Service members who worked in environments with above-average rates of sexual harassment against their colleagues were approximately twice as likely to be sexually assaulted than were service members who worked where such rates were below average. In models that included individual-level predictors of sexual assault risk (e.g., date of birth, occupational group, and prior sexual assault victimization), ambient sexual harassment continued to contribute significantly to sexual assault risk. After we controlled for a wide array of risk factors, we found that service members were at the highest risk of sexual assault in the environments in which other colleagues had a high risk of being sexually harassed.

This study is correlational and cannot empirically determine the precise causal pathways that give rise to the observed association. Generally speaking, ambient sexual harassment might directly cause sexual assault risk (or vice versa). Alternatively, both might be caused by a common factor that was not among the risk factors we controlled for. For example, a direct causal link implies that stopping instances of sexual harassment would directly prevent subsequent sexual assaults. This could occur if some assault perpetrators begin with sexual harassment and then escalate to more-serious behaviors when they are not stopped. Similarly, it could occur because individuals who observe that sexual harassment is common in their environments come to believe that sexual assault is also common or unlikely to be punished, increasing their likelihood of perpetrating an assault. Alternatively, the association could occur because of some other factor in a service member's environment that makes both sexual assault and harassment more likely. For example, there could be a culture or leadership style in some units or at some installations that makes both sexual assault and harassment more likely. Or perhaps both assault and harassment are facilitated by some aspect of the physical environment, such as living on a ship or in barracks in close quarters. It is quite possible that the association between sexual harassment and sexual assault occurs for multiple reasons, including both direct effects and the effects of cultural or environmental factors. However, we do not have to know the precise causal relations that give rise to the observed association in order to draw some broad conclusions from these findings.

First, *sexual assault and sexual harassment in the military should be thought of as resulting from a single problem or as a single underlying workplace disorder.* This view is consistent with the Centers for Disease Control and Prevention's continuum of harm model (Centers for Disease Control and Prevention, 2004), which was adopted in DoD's *2014–2016 Sexual Assault Prevention Strategy* (DoD, 2014). In the strategy document, both sexual assault and sexual harassment are considered to exist on a single dimension of harmful sexualized workplace behavior. The difference between the two is that assault is on the higher end of this continuum of harm, and harassment is generally lower; in addition, some inappropriate sexual behaviors (e.g., jokes) may be still lower on the continuum of harm if they do not meet the legal definition of harassment. Behaviors that are lower on the continuum are seen as creating an environment that supports not only inappropriate workplace behavior and sexual harassment but also sexual assault. Because behaviors across the continuum are seen as driven by the same underlying root causes, a holistic prevention strategy may be necessary (as opposed to focusing on the most extreme end of the continuum). Indeed, DoD's *Prevention Plan of Action: 2019–2023* (Office of the Under Secretary of Defense for Personnel and Readiness, 2019) recommends a comprehensive approach to prevention and encourages collaboration across the military system to jointly address risk factors that are shared across different destructive behaviors.

Our view that sexual assault and harassment should be conceptualized as representing a single underlying disorder is also consistent with other findings from studies of the military. For example, military sexual assaults against men are often perpetrated for hazing purposes rather than sexual gratification (Jaycox et al., 2015), and both the perpetrators and victims may experience such events as a form of harassment rather than sexual assault. Similarly, research has shown that service members who are sexual minorities are at substantially increased risk of sexual assault (Davis, Vega, and McLeod, 2017), which suggests that sexual assault is tied to sexual orientation discrimination. Finally, some victims report that the assaults were preceded by harassment by the same perpetrators. According to results from the 2014 RMWS survey, one-third of service members who were sexually assaulted indicated that their perpetrator sexually harassed them before the assault, and 9 percent indicated that the perpetrator(s) stalked them before the assault (Jaycox et al., 2015). Thus, the view that sexual harassment and sexual assault reflect the same underlying disorder is consistent with a wide range of empirical findings. These twin problems often happen to the same individuals repeatedly, and they are often carried out by the same perpetrators; even when sexual harassment and sexual assault happen to different individuals, they tend to co-occur in the same units, installations, and major commands. In addition, the majority of sexual assaults of service members also meet the legal definition of sexual harassment.

A second broad conclusion that we can draw is that *efforts to prevent sexual assault should emphasize preventing or stopping sexual harassment.* Viewing sexual harassment as existing on the same continuum as sexual assault suggests the need for novel sexual assault prevention programs. Even in the civilian sector, such programs have had disappointingly small effects on the number of sexual assaults among college students (Anderson and Whiston, 2005). Programs that can prevent sexual harassment, or stop ongoing sexual harassment, may prevent actions that fall on the higher end of the harm continuum. Currently, the military programs to prevent and respond to sexual harassment are underdeveloped relative to prevention efforts targeting sexual assault. For example, at most installations, there are few or no personnel tasked with preventing or responding to harassment, although there are such individuals tasked with addressing sexual assault. Thus, there is usually no one responsible for following up with the victim to ensure that the harassment stopped and that the victim has not experienced retaliation. Although military leaders are required to report sexual assault to an investigative authority, they have no obligation to report sexual harassment when they become aware of it; indeed, there is currently no system to accept such reports. There is no standard mechanism by which information about the perpetration of sexual harassment is entered into personnel records, made available to subsequent commanders, or made available to subsequent investigators. This suggests that there may be room for improvement in military sexual harassment prevention efforts, particularly by treating sexual harassment as a more serious infraction than is currently the case.

Given the frequent overlap of sexual harassment and sexual assault, one might expect that they would share similar prevention and response systems. However, with the exception of those in the Army system, the individuals responsible for providing prevention training, providing victim advocacy and services, and adjudicating the administrative or criminal response to offenders are distinct (U.S. Government Accountability Office, 2017; Marquis et al., 2017). Furthermore, researcher and policy experts typically focus on only one of the two areas. This might be partially an artifact of the perpetrator response system, in which sexual harassment is a civil offense and sexual assault is a criminal offense. Nonetheless, there appears to be no strong rationale that requires primary prevention training to be delivered distinctly or the victim response systems to be distinct. For example, the confidential reporting system that allows sexual assault victims to document the event and to privately seek advocacy, mental health, and physical health services could be a useful model for sexual harassment victims who may also benefit from a similar approach. Further research and analysis that investigates shared causal factors and recommends shared prevention and response strategies could be helpful in guiding the direction of the DoD response.

There are also some practical reasons to believe that targeting sexual misconduct that is lower on the continuum of harm may be easier than targeting sexual assault directly. Sexual harassment behaviors are more visible than sexual assault (i.e., they often occur in shared environments where there are witnesses) and, therefore, are more easily sanctioned. In contrast, sexual assaults typically occur in private with only the victim and perpetrator present. There are many more opportunities for colleagues to deliver social sanctions that communicate the unacceptability of the sexual harassment and for supervisors and commanders to deliver professional sanctions. Because sexual harassment can span from minor, inappropriate behavior to repeated, severe sexual harassment, there are also opportunities to sanction sexual harassment while the consequences are still relatively mild and more easily delivered. Sexual assault is a crime, and delivering a criminal punishment requires proof beyond a reasonable doubt; however, this level of proof is often not available in such cases. In contrast, the punishments for sexual harassment are administrative and do not require such a high evidentiary standard. As a result, a reported harassment should be more likely to result in sanctions to the perpetrator than would an accusation of sexual assault.

In addition, because sexual harassment solutions could be limited to peer-delivered social sanctions or supervisor-controlled professional sanctions, the timeline for delivery can be quite fast compared with the timeline of sanctions for sexual assault delivered by the military justice system. The likelihood that a person will learn from an event and modify his or her behavior in response to a sanction increases when the punishment occurs quickly (Schwartz, Wasserman, and Robbins, 2001). Thus, paradoxically, because sexual harassment is lower on the continuum of harm, it is possible for punishment to be more certain to occur and to occur more quickly than it would for cases of sexual assault.

We believe that our analyses point to the promise of reducing or eliminating workplace sexual harassment as a strategy to also prevent sexual assault. This study also provides supportive evidence for DoD's policy focus on the continuum of harm in sexual assault prevention planning. The true test will come after high-quality programs or policies to improve workplace culture are delivered to a large segment of the military population; once those are in place, researchers can conduct a real-world test of the programs' and policies' influence on sexual harassment in the work environment and, finally, on sexual assault risk.

Smoothing Ambient Sexual Harassment Values for Small Units

In this appendix, we describe our process to reduce variance in ambient sexual harassment rates, especially among small units. For each gender, we added K pseudo-observations to each unit, with sexual harassment set equal to the service-gender prevalence. Unit ambient sexual harassment against men is derived as follows: Let y_i be the sexual harassment measure for RMWS respondent i, let c_{it} be the unit identification code of individual i in month t, and let S_i be the service branch for individual i. Furthermore, let M_i be an indicator that service member i is male. Then, the smoothed exposure to ambient sexual harassment against men for service member i at month t is given by the following equation:

$$uic^m_{it,K} = \frac{1}{K + \left\|I^m_{it}\right\|_0}\left(K\hat{p}_{S_i} + \sum_{j \in I^m_{it}} y_j\right),$$

where $I^m_{it} = \{j: C_{jt} = C_{it}, M_j = 1, j \neq i\}$ is the set of men in the same unit as service member i in month t, excluding service member i; $\left\|I^m_{it}\right\|_0$ is the number of service members in the set; and $\hat{p}_{S_i}$ is the prevalence of sexual harassment against men in service S_i.

The overall smoothed ambient sexual harassment against men at the unit level for service member i is then a simple average over the study period:

$$uic^m_{i,K} = \frac{1}{12}\sum_{t=1}^{12} uic^m_{it,K}.$$

Note that some service members did not have 12 months of observations. In such cases, this average was taken over the observed months in service.

This same methodology applies to the derivation of ambient sexual harassment against men and women and to each level of the environment (unit, based on unit identification code; installation, based on zip or postal code; and major command, based on major command or monitored command code). Let $uic^f_{i,K}$ denote the smoothed ambient sexual harassment against women for service member i at the unit level with smoothing K. Let $zip_{i,K}^{m}$, $zip_{i,K}^{f}$, $mcc_{i,K}^{m}$, and $mcc_{i,K}^{f}$ be defined similarly, but at the installation zip code and major command levels. To combine these various ambient environments, a simple average is taken within individual

$$SH_{i,K}^{m} = \frac{uic_{i,K}^{m} + zip_{i,K}^{m} + mcc_{i,K}^{m}}{3}$$

and

$$SH_{i,K}^{f} = \frac{uic_{i,K}^{f} + zip_{i,K}^{f} + mcc_{i,K}^{f}}{3}.$$

To determine the optimal smoothing parameter K, a model is fit predicting sexual assault risk using these two ambient sexual harassment measures. We fit the following weighted logistic regression separately for each service-by-gender (eight models total):

$$\text{logit}(\text{Pr}(SA_i = 1)) = \beta_0 + \beta_1 SH_{i,K}^{m} + \beta_2 SH_{i,K}^{f},$$

with RMWS case weights previously derived to adjust for sampling and nonresponse (see Morral, Gore, and Schell, 2014). Using these model fits, we choose a value of K that maximizes the likelihood function. Figure A.1 depicts the number of pseudo-observations at each log-likelihood. The log-likelihood begins to flatten out at around $K = 15$ and reaches a maximum at $K = 24$. This illustrates that there is a substantial benefit to smoothing smaller environments to the service-gender prevalence.

Figure A.1
Log-Likelihood as a Function of the Number of Pseudo-Observations Added to Each Unit, with Sexual Harassment Equal to the Service-Gender Prevalence

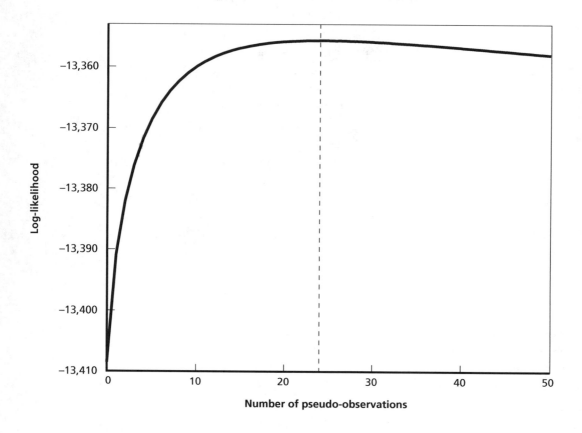

References

Anderson, Linda A., and Susan C. Whiston, "Sexual Assault Education Programs: A Meta-Analytic Examination of Their Effectiveness," *Psychology of Women Quarterly*, Vol. 29, No. 4, 2005, pp. 374–388.

Buchanan, NiCole T., Isis H. Settles, and Krystle C. Woods, "Comparing Sexual Harassment Subtypes Among Black and White Women by Military Rank: Double Jeopardy, the Jezebel, and the Cult of True Womanhood," *Psychology of Women Quarterly*, Vol. 32, No. 4, 2008, pp. 347–361.

Centers for Disease Control and Prevention, *Sexual Violence Prevention: Beginning the Dialogue*, Atlanta, Ga., 2004.

Davis, Lisa, Ronald P. Vega, and Jeffrey McLeod, "Additional Descriptive Analyses and Future Directions," in Lisa Davis, Amanda Grifka, Kristin Williams, and Margaret Coffey, eds., *2016 Workplace and Gender Relations Survey of Active Duty Members: Overview Report*, Alexandria, Va.: U.S. Department of Defense, Office of People Analytics, Report No. 2016-050, May 2017, pp. 355–367.

Defense Manpower Data Center, *2010 Workplace and Gender Relations Survey of Active Duty Members: Overview Report on Sexual Assault*, Arlington, Va., Report No. 2010-025, 2011.

———, "2012 Workplace and Gender Relations Survey of Active Duty Members," Arlington, Va., Survey Note No. 2013-007, March 15, 2013.

DoD—*See* U.S. Department of Defense.

Farris, Coreen, Lisa H. Jaycox, Terry L. Schell, Amy E. Street, Dean G. Kilpatrick, and Terri Tanielian, "Sexual Harassment and Gender Discrimination Findings: Active Component," in Andrew R. Morral, Kristie L. Gore, and Terry L. Schell, eds., *Sexual Assault and Sexual Harassment in the U.S. Military: Volume 2. Estimates for Department of Defense Service Members from the 2014 RAND Military Workplace Study*, Santa Monica, Calif.: RAND Corporation, RR-870/2-1-OSD, 2015, pp. 31–54. As of July 25, 2019:
https://www.rand.org/pubs/research_reports/RR870z2-1.html

Fitzgerald, Louise F., Fritz Drasgow, Charles L. Hulin, Michele J. Gelfand, and Vicki J. Magley, "Antecedents and Consequences of Sexual Harassment in Organizations: A Test of an Integrated Model," *Journal of Applied Psychology*, Vol. 82, No. 4, 1997, pp. 578–589.

Glomb, T. M., W. L. Richman, C. L. Hulin, F. Drasgow, K. T. Schneider, and L. F. Fitzgerald, "Ambient Sexual Harassment: An Integrated Model of Antecedents and Consequences," *Organizational Behavior and Human Decision Processes*, Vol. 71, No. 3, 1997, pp. 309–328.

Harned, Melanie S., Alayne J. Ormerod, Patrick A. Palmieri, Linda L. Collinsworth, and Maggie Reed, "Sexual Assault by Workplace Personnel and Other Types of Sexual Harassment: A Comparison of Antecedents and Consequences," *Journal of Occupational Health Psychology*, Vol. 7, No. 2, 2002, pp. 174–188.

Harris, Richard, *Sexism, Sexual Harassment and Sexual Assault: Toward Conceptual Clarity*, Patrick Air Force Base, Fla.: Defense Equal Opportunity Management Institute, Report Number 07-01, Summer 2007.

Harris, Richard J., Daniel P. McDonald, and Corey S. Sparks, "Sexual Harassment in the Military: Individual Experiences, Demographics, and Organizational Contexts," *Armed Forces and Society*, Vol. 44, No. 1, 2018, pp. 25–43.

Jaycox, Lisa H., Terry L. Schell, Andrew R. Morral, Amy Street, Coreen Farris, Dean Kilpatrick, and Terri Tanielian, "Sexual Assault Findings: Active Component," in Andrew R. Morral, Kristie L. Gore, and Terry L. Schell, eds., *Sexual Assault and Sexual Harassment in the U.S. Military: Volume 2. Estimates for Department of Defense Service Members from the 2014 RAND Military Workplace Study*, Santa Monica, Calif.: RAND Corporation, RR-870/2-1-OSD, 2015, pp. 9–30. As of July 25, 2019: https://www.rand.org/pubs/research_reports/RR870z2-1.html

Kimerling, Rachel, Kristian Gima, Mark W. Smith, Amy Street, and Susan Frayne, "The Veterans Health Administration and Military Sexual Trauma," *American Journal of Public Health*, Vol. 97, No. 12, 2007, pp. 2160–2166.

LeardMann, C. A., A. Pietrucha, K. M. Magruder, B. Smith, M. Murdoch, I. G. Jacobson, M. A. K. Ryan, G. Gackstetter, T. C. Smith, and Millennium Cohort Study Team, "Combat Deployment Is Associated with Sexual Harassment or Sexual Assault in a Large, Female Military Cohort," *Women's Health Issues*, Vol. 23, No. 4, 2013, pp. e215–e223.

Marquis, Jefferson P., Coreen Farris, Kimberly Curry Hall, Kristy N. Kamarck, Nelson Lim, Douglas Shontz, Paul S. Steinberg, Robert Stewart, Thomas E. Trail, Jennie W. Wenger, Anny Wong, and Eunice C. Wong, *Improving Oversight and Coordination of Department of Defense Programs That Address Problematic Behaviors Among Military Personnel: Final Report*, Santa Monica, Calif.: RAND Corporation, RR-1352-OSD, 2017. As of July 25, 2019: https://www.rand.org/pubs/research_reports/RR1352.html

Morral, Andrew R., Kristie L. Gore, and Terry L. Schell, eds., *Sexual Assault and Sexual Harassment in the U.S. Military: Volume 1. Design of the 2014 RAND Military Workplace Study*, Santa Monica, Calif.: RAND Corporation, RR-870/1-OSD, 2014. As of July 25, 2019: https://www.rand.org/pubs/research_reports/RR870z1.html

———, eds., *Sexual Assault and Sexual Harassment in the U.S. Military: Volume 2. Estimates for Department of Defense Service Members from the 2014 RAND Military Workplace Study*, Santa Monica, Calif.: RAND Corporation, RR-870/2-1-OSD, 2015. As of July 25, 2019: https://www.rand.org/pubs/research_reports/RR870z2-1.html

———, eds., *Sexual Assault and Sexual Harassment in the U.S. Military: Volume 4. Investigations of Potential Bias in Estimates from the 2014 RAND Military Workplace Study*, Santa Monica, Calif.: RAND Corporation, RR-870/6-OSD, 2016. As of July 25, 2019: https://www.rand.org/pubs/research_reports/RR870z6.html

Moral, Andrew R., Terry L. Schell, Matthew Cefalu, Jessica Hwang, and Andrew Gelman, *Sexual Assault and Sexual Harassment in the U.S. Military: Volume 5. Estimates for Installation- and Command-Level Risk of Sexual Assault and Sexual Harassment from the 2014 RAND Military Workplace Study*, Santa Monica, Calif.: RAND Corporation, RR-870/7-OSD, 2018. As of July 25, 2019: https://www.rand.org/pubs/research_reports/RR870z7.html

Morral, Andrew R., Terry L. Schell, and Kristie L. Gore, "Discussion and Recommendations," in Andrew R. Morral, Kristie L. Gore, and Terry L. Schell, eds., *Sexual Assault and Sexual Harassment in the U.S. Military: Volume 2. Estimates for Department of Defense Service Members from the 2014 RAND Military Workplace Study*, Santa Monica, Calif.: RAND Corporation, RR-870/2-1-OSD, 2015, pp. 87–99. As of July 25, 2019: https://www.rand.org/pubs/research_reports/RR870z2-1.html

Office of the Under Secretary of Defense for Personnel and Readiness, *Prevention Plan of Action: 2019–2023*, Washington, D.C.: U.S. Department of Defense, April 2019.

Raver, J. L., and M. J. Gelfand, "Beyond the Individual Victim: Linking Sexual Harassment, Team Processes, and Team Performance," *Academy of Management Journal*, Vol. 48, No. 3, 2005, pp. 387–400.

Richman-Hirsch, W. L., and T. M. Glomb, "Are Men Affected by the Sexual Harassment of Women? Effects of Ambient Sexual Harassment on Men," in J. M Brett and F. Drasgow, eds., *Psychology of Work: Theoretically Based Empirical Research*, Mahwah, N.J.: Lawrence Erlbaum, 2002, pp. 121–140.

Sadler, Anne G., Brenda M. Booth, Brian L. Cook, and Bradley N. Doebbeling, "Factors Associated with Women's Risk of Rape in the Military Environment," *American Journal of Industrial Medicine*, Vol. 43, No. 3, 2003, pp. 262–273.

Schell, Terry L., and Andrew R. Morral, "Branch of Service Differences in the Rates of Sexual Assault and Sexual Harassment," in Andrew R. Morral, Kristie L. Gore, and Terry L. Schell, eds., *Sexual Assault and Sexual Harassment in the U.S. Military: Volume 2. Estimates for Department of Defense Service Members from the 2014 RAND Military Workplace Study*, Santa Monica, Calif.: RAND Corporation, RR-870/2-1-OSD, 2015a, pp. 61–68. As of July 25, 2019: https://www.rand.org/pubs/research_reports/RR870z2-1.html

———, "Findings from the Reserve Component," in Andrew R. Morral, Kristie L. Gore, and Terry L. Schell, eds., *Sexual Assault and Sexual Harassment in the U.S. Military: Volume 2. Estimates for Department of Defense Service Members from the 2014 RAND Military Workplace Study*, Santa Monica, Calif.: RAND Corporation, RR-870/2-1-OSD, 2015b, pp. 77–85. As of July 25, 2019: https://www.rand.org/pubs/research_reports/RR870z2-1.html

Schell, Terry L., Andrew R. Morral, Matthew Cefalu, Coreen Farris, and Miriam Matthews, *Risk Factors for Sexual Assault and Sexual Harassment in the U.S. Military: Findings from the 2014 RAND Military Workplace Study*, Santa Monica, Calif.: RAND Corporation, RR-870/9-OSD, forthcoming.

Schneider, Kimberly Taylor, *Bystander Stress: The Effect of Organizational Tolerance of Sexual Harassment on Victims' Coworkers*, dissertation, Champaign, Ill.: University of Illinois, Urbana-Champaign, 1996.

Schwartz, B., E. A. Wasserman, and S. J. Robbins, *Psychology of Learning and Behavior*, New York: Norton, 2001.

Street, Amy E., Jaimie L. Gradus, Jane Stafford, and Kacie Kelly, "Gender Differences in Experiences of Sexual Harassment: Data from a Male-Dominated Environment," *Journal of Consulting and Clinical Psychology*, Vol. 75, No. 3, 2007, pp. 464–474.

Street, Amy E., Anthony J. Rosellini, Robert J. Ursano, Steven G. Heeringa, Eric D. Hill, John Monahan, James A. Naifeh, Maria V. Petukhova, Ben Y. Reis, Nancy A. Sampson, Paul D. Bliese, Murray B. Stein, Alan M. Zaslavsky, and Ronald C. Kessler, "Developing a Risk Model to Target High-Risk Preventive Interventions for Sexual Assault Victimization Among Female U.S. Army Soldiers," *Clinical Psychological Science*, Vol. 4, No. 6, 2016, pp. 939–956.

Street, Amy E., Jane Stafford, Clare M. Mahan, and Ann Hendricks, "Sexual Harassment and Assault Experienced by Reservists During Military Service: Prevalence and Health Correlates," *Journal of Rehabilitation Research and Development*, Vol. 45, No. 3, 2008, pp. 409–419.

U.S. Department of Defense, *Sexual Assault Prevention and Response (SAPR) Program*, Washington, D.C., DoD Directive 6495.01, January 23, 2012, incorporating change 1, April 30, 2013.

———, *2014–2016 Sexual Assault Prevention Strategy*, Washington, D.C., April 30, 2014.

———, *Department of Defense Military Equal Opportunity (MEO) Program*, Washington, D.C., DoD Directive 1350.2, August 18, 1995, incorporating change 2, June 8, 2015.

U.S. Government Accountability Office, *Sexual Violence: Actions Needed to Improve DoD's Efforts to Address the Continuum of Unwanted Sexual Behaviors*, Washington, D.C., GAO-18-33, December 2017.